Words of Comfort from the Heart

MISS JERRY LEE SCHOCK

Words of Comfort from the Heart

Copyright © 2021 by Miss Jerry Lee Schock.

Paperback ISBN: 978-1-63812-166-4
Ebook ISBN: 978-1-63812-167-1

All rights reserved. No part in this book may be produced and transmitted in any form or by any means, electronic, or mechanical, including photocopying, recording, or by any information storage and retrieval system, without permission in writing from the copyright owner.

The views expressed in this work are solely those of the author and do not necessarily reflect the views of the publisher hereby disclaims any responsibility for them.

Published by Pen Culture Solutions   12/10/2021

Pen Culture Solutions
1-888-727-7204 (USA)
1-800-950-458 (Australia)
support@penculturesolutions.com

The book *"Words of Comfort from the Heart"* is a beautiful collection of poems that will give you inspiration and uplift your spirit. I even feel blessed after reading the book and that gives me a lot of encouragement to keep going with my life. The Author knows how to comfort her audiences with each poem that she wrote. This is also another great book that I do recommend. – Alex Sanders

Contents

1. A Loved One Has Crossed Over ... 1
2. A Mother's Heart ... 2
3. As They Wait ... 3
4. As We Wait ... 4
5. Balm Of Protection ... 5
6. Full of Grace ... 6
7. He is Home ... 7
8. Heaven is Sweeter ... 8
9. Her Light Still Shines ... 9
10. His Arms of Love ... 10
11. His Journey ... 11
12. Home Before Nightfall ... 12
13. I Am Waiting ... 13
14. I Can Hear Miss Nellie-Say ... 15
15. I Have Watched ... 16
16. In Loving Memory of Mommy ... 17
17. In Loving Memory of Morris Lamb ... 23
18. In Loving Memory of our Sister Linda Garcia ... 24
19. It Seems So Soon ... 25
20. I've Watched You ... 26
21. Mothers ... 27
22. My Heart Cries Out ... 28
23. My Heart Is Heavy ... 29
24. One Day ... 30
25. Our Hearts Are Broken ... 31
26. Our Mother's ... 33
27. Remembering Theresa Beuchler ... 34
28. She Went to Sleep ... 35
29. She's Gone On ... 36

30. Someone to Lead 37
31. Sympathy Short Poems..38
32. The Burden..39
33. The Burden is Heavy..40
34. The Garden..41
35. The Homegoing 42
36. The Long Road..43
37. The Loved One's He Has Taken 44
38. The Pain, The Peace 45
39. The Path...46
40. The Struggle 47
41. The Whisper of Her Wings..48
42. Their Sacrifice...49
43. There's A Road Ahead 50
44. To Comfort You In Sorrow 51
45. Tomorrow or Today...52
46. We Said Goodbye..53
47. What A Precious Angel 54
48. When We Can Do No More 55
49. With Deepest Sympathy..56
50. With Heartfelt Sympathy 57
51. Wits End 58

A Loved One Has Crossed Over

They knew the time would come, when they would have to say goodbye,
And their hearts are truly broken, as for their loved one they cry.
But Lord we know that life and death are truly in Your Hands,
And You have this sweet girl with You, that was Your Master plan.
Their lives will seem so empty as they journey on their way,
But peace and strength will come from You, with each new passing day.
The memories they all will have of times that now are past,
Will bring a smile as they think of her and times they shared will last.
She is in Heaven now, and Jesus was waiting for her there,
As He guided her safely over, to her Heavenly home so fair.
No more suffering, and no more pain, will she ever feel again,
And someday soon we'll meet her, waiting for us, with Him.

Given to me by the Lord
Jerry L Schock
05/09/2016

A Mother's Heart

When a mother's heart is aching, o'er a child that's gone astray,
It's a hurt that goes much deeper than any words can say.
It's a pain for which only the Lord can bring relief.
A pain that overtakes the mind, sometimes beyond belief.
We can only turn to You Lord, to help us through the trial ,
Knowing peace that passes understanding, will come after a while.
You have those prayer warriors who will intercession make,
As they, our every need, before Your throne will take.
Father I would ask of You, to heal the broken heart;
Strengthen it through every hour until the pain departs.
Help a mother look to Heaven, even though her heart will bleed,
Let her know that You are still the supplier of every need.
Touch the child who's gone astray, and trouble that dear mind;
Take the fetters from their eyes, that make them oh so blind;
Renew the truths they know from You, deep inside their heart,
'Til through Your precious wooing, they will from sin depart.

Jerry L Schock
1/2/00

As They Wait

As they wait -watching their loved one-helpless are they all-
Praying for Your touch-as on Your Name they call-
Oh Father wrap each one close in Your arms of love-
As they wait and wonder when she'll go to Heaven above.
There is nothing we can do but pray for strength and peace-
Until at last at home with You- she finds sweet relief.

For Miss Bertha 's family
from Miss Jerry
02/25/07

As We Wait

He's on his way to Heaven as they wait beside his bed-
Never did we think of this, but by Your Hand we're led.
We do not want to see him suffer or be in terrible pain,
But Father we seek Your will and ask Your glory to gain.
His life reflects all Your goodness and his legacy is grace.
With the death angel ever near-he longs to see Your face.
We pray for peace and protection for all that we hold dear-
And ask You bring them comfort and wash away the fear.
We praise You for Your goodness and for mercy and grace,
As we follow where You lead, and seek that special place.

Given to me by the Lord
Jerry L Schock
8/14/2019

Balm Of Protection

Today there's a balm of protection
easing some of the pain-
We know that earth's loss,
is surely Heavens gain.
Tomorrow and in days ahead
the reality will be known,
Mama's no longer with us and
yet we're not alone.
Though we can't reach out and touch
the one we've loved for many years
We'll remember all her love and
smile through the tears.
Our hearts are saddened-but
For us you see
For in Heaven there is now
A jubilee.

With love,
Miss Jerry

Full of Grace

As I watch my precious sister-and see her smiling face,
I know afresh dear Lord –You've filled her full of grace.
As the word came that You had called her precious Mother home-
I prayed You'd surround her with angels –and she'd never feel alone-
I prayed for grace and peace beyond all measure from above-
And see the answer to those prayers –as she shows forth Your love.
Thank You precious Father for every answered prayer-
Hold her very close and keep her in Your care.

With Love
Miss Jerry

He is Home

What can we say Lord? We knew the day would come,
When suffering would end and You would call him home.
It was never in our minds that he would leave so fast-
And yet in the midst of the pain, we know he's home at last.
We say he was much too young and this should never be-
But our lives are in Your hands-the future we cannot see.
If we were to see trouble ahead then we would often fret-
In facing the unknown with You as guide-every need is met.
Angels surround each of us-when You call a loved one home-
And You give us peace and comfort to know we're not alone.
You've guided many a loved one –safe to the other shore;
And we know one day we'll be there-with You
forevermore.

In Loving memory of
Wayne Sweat
Jerry L Schock
8/16/08

Heaven is Sweeter

Heaven sure is sweeter, our brother made it home,
Thank You precious Father, he did not go on alone.
The angels stood by his bed waiting, until it was time–
As Jesus stepped out and said –he's here, he's mine.
He served You with a passion not many have today.
He knew when sickness came and death was on the way–
That all was in Your hands and You were by his side–
He started looking for Jesus knowing in You he'd abide.
The grace that You have given was present from the start–
And he knew that he was safe with Jesus in his heart.
He sang nothing but praises for You until the very end–
And when he crossed the river –he found his dearest friend.

In Loving memory of
Wayne Sweat
Jerry L Schock
8/3/08

Her Light Still Shines

Miss Nellie's gone to Heaven, and life will never be the same,
Yet Lord we're so much richer for the lessons we have gained.
She taught her children well, and loved her husband true,
But the center of all she did, our precious Lord was You.
Every time the choir sang, "I Was Born to Serve the Lord",
Miss Nellie's image was in our minds –of her reading the Word.
She was such a precious angel, as beside her husband she'd walk;
And in each conversation was praise for You, every time she'd talk..
The light that shown around her daily came from very deep within-
Now that light shines bright in Heaven –but on earth it will never dim.
The legacy she leaves behind is one of truth and Jesus' love-
A message that is never-ending-sent from Heaven above.
Lord You know we are so grateful for the little time we had;
But we are sure -You understand- within our hearts we are sad.
Her voice is stilled upon the earth but in Heaven it clearly rings-
Her praises for You will never end –as with Your choir she sings.

For Miss Nellie's family
–as we mourn our loss, and celebrate Heaven's gain.
Jerry L. Schock
12/25/10

His Arms of Love

By Jerry L. Schock

The angels walk beside Him today, as He carries you through this trial
And with His tender care and love, you'll find healing after a while,
His arms are wrapped around you as they shield you from the storm
They draw you close to His breast –and protect you from all harm.
I know at times it is dark and you may not see the light on that shore
But Jesus is loving and keeping you near, until you can stand once more.
His promises will not fail you, you need never feel you're all alone;
For, the Father up in Heaven always will love and care for His own.

Jerry L.Schock
10/26/2016

His Journey

He spent so many years driving up and down the road-
Carrying a burden for the lost-tho'not a part of his load.
He'd share his Jesus willingly with everyone he'd meet-
Whether on the road-or walking down the street-
He always came to church and spent much time in prayer-
Grateful each and every time-someone brought him there-
He praised the Lord for goodness and grace beyond compare-
Even in the pain-you'd still find him sitting in that chair-
He's been ready to go home for such a long, long time-
And openly let those near him know, for Heaven he did pine.
Today his journey is over –and pain's a thing of the past-
He went to meet his Savior-and is now at rest at last.
God gave us many precious years and memories are sweet-
Wait by the gate my brother-for someday soon we'll meet.

In loving memory of Bro. Strange
With Love,
Miss Jerry
04/02/07

Home Before Nightfall

Miss Nellie prayed

I wanted to go before night fall, and all memory was gone-
The Father answered my prayers, because I could not go on.
My body has grown so weary and my mind is growing dim,
   So let Jesus please come get me –so I can be with Him.
Right now there is such a sadness, you think will never end,
But you'll have the sweetest memories fill your hearts again.
The Savior has promised faithfully-you will never be alone-
Remember those promises daily, you are not on Your own.
   My presence will hover nearby-in everything you do,
I know the valley is not forever, and Jesus is holding you.

For Miss Nellie's Family
Jerry L Schock
From the Lord 12/28/10

I Am Waiting

Don't weep for me, children of mine-
don't be sad today.
I'm at rest now with my Lord-
safe in His arms to stay.

Part of me did not want to go-
as you waited through the storm,
But my trip became so easy
when the angels took me home.

I'm waiting now on Heavens shore
and in just a little while-
I'll meet you there with loved ones,
you'll know the reason I smile.

I served Him such a long time,
His Word I hid in my heart-
But I knew the day would come
when we would have to part.

I saw those eyes of love,
as I stepped on Heaven's shore
And knew I was free from the
pains of life forevermore.

Even though God let me suffer
He brought me through the pain-
As I desired others to see Him,
and peace and comfort to gain.

Remember when you think of me,
I don't want you to be sad-
But think I've just gone home-
and I'm waiting for you with dad.

Given to me by the Lord for Ellen and her family
As Miss Johnnie waits for us
Jerry L Schock
7/22/2000

I Can Hear Miss Nellie-Say

I can hear Miss Nellie-say from up on Heavens shore:
Don't weep my precious loved ones-I am safe forevermore.
My love for you will never die, you will never be alone.
Remember lessons I taught you-while you were at home-
Remember to love each other-and stay very close to the Lord;
Walk the straight and narrow way, depending on His Word.
Remember all the good times and the fun we always had,
Be sure to look after each other, especially your Dad.
He took good care of us and preached the Word so true,
Now he needs extra comfort, that can only come from you.
Be true to all I taught you and share freely of your love,
And very soon I'll meet you all in Heaven up above.

Given to me by the Lord for the Moore Family
Jerry L Schock
12/27/10

I Have Watched

I've watched as Satan's fought you time and time again;
Yet I've seen you turn your eyes to Heaven, and to Him.
I've watched as things have happened that would surely break apart,
The love of many a Christian and yet you've set your heart.
You've turned your eyes to Jesus; you've given Him the praise,
You've suffered many, many things in these past few days.
And yet the Lord has strengthened and brought you closer still.
Oh Lord, build a hedge of thorns, as You do Your precious will.
I ask that You would take each one and draw them close to You,
Soothe the pain they're feeling now, do what only You can do.
Father You've given me a special love for every one of them,
Jerry and Jeremy and Lisa and precious little Robin.
My precious Heavenly Father, may Your perfect will be done,
But Lord I know their hearts are broken, each and every one.
I ask you now to mend them, quickly, as days go by,
I ask that You will comfort them, for Lord, we can't know why.
I pray that You will give a peace as only You can do
As the hedge of thorns grows higher, from Heaven and You.
I pray You will protect them, wrap them in Your arms of love
Send those guardian angels, very quickly from above.
He's given us many comforts He has the right to take away.
To the Lord be praise and glory; Now and ever, let us pray.

Given to me by the Lord
9/7/1996
Jerry L Schock

In Loving Memory of Mommy

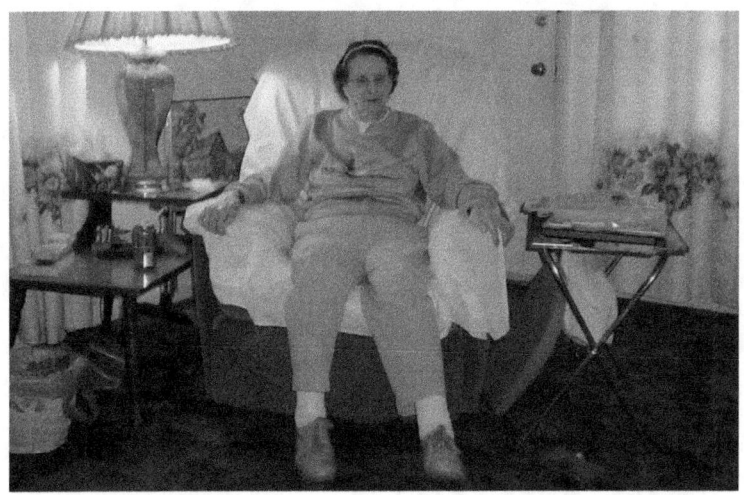

Mommy you've gone to Heaven to meet your Savior there,
Far removed from pain, and all this earthly care.
God gave you many years –to help us learn and grow,
Filling us with love, teaching the way to go.
You taught us with a faith that time can never take away -
And said the Lord would provide each and every day.
Things were not always easy for you on the path of life-
But the faith you had in God carried you through the strife.
You always found time to play and the memories are sweet-
Remembering all the fun -like skating down the street.
We bowled and played baseball and enjoyed all we did-
As you made time for each of us- loving every kid.
We knew the time would come when we'd have to part-
What an empty place it leaves deep within our heart.
Your love surrounds us now each and every day-
And will carry us through life-helping us not to stray-

You saw us through all the heartaches life would bring-
And the I love you's that we heard- in our ears still ring.
Life's lessons have been learned in the time we had with you,
And only Heaven will reveal the rewards God has it's true-
For such a loving Mother –who sacrificed so much-
Ensuring each and every one of us felt your loving touch.

In loving memory of our Mom-
Ada Lee Schock
5/10/1921 to 7/19/2011
By Jerry Lee Schock
7/24/11

August 6, 2011

You went to Heaven on July 19th, 2011 –not that long ago but so long. I still want to call you at the end of the day –but you are not where any of us can phone you. Somehow, I think you are still watching over us-because of all the love I feel every time I think of something you said, which is all the time. It hurts but there is a peace knowing that love and those life lessons you taught are ours forever. You will never be far from us.

I can remember in the early years with Jerry in the stroller and Stan on one side and me on the other- walking across the grass to go to Sunday School at the Lutheran Church. Early you began to plant the seeds of faith. When times would get rough and you were not sure how things would work out -I can still hear you say- "the darkest hour is just before dawn-things will work out" and they always did.

You worked 3 jobs to keep us together despite your own Mother telling you it was not possible to raise 3 kids alone. How many times you would say that you were not raising us alone-but God was with you.

How many times I heard you say as decisions were made "God did not give you kids to me to keep-He only loaned you to me to teach you the right way and then let you go when you are grown and trust those lessons to carry you through life." How those words brought comfort as I buried my own child.

I can remember a red headed woman throwing herself over Grandpa Herman's coffin as we prepared to bury him and asking what was wrong with her. Another life lesson-"that is because she treated him terrible when he was alive-if you treat people right when they are with you-there are no regrets when they are gone". How many times we were told to apologize to others -even when we were not in the wrong. Another of Mom's lessons learned. Never let the sun set on your anger. Heal it before it festers-make it right because you never know if those will be the last words you speak to that person-anything can happen and you never want your last words to be angry –there are no regrets that way."

You taught us all very early in life to love and say I love you, as you led by example–and as we grew older you made sure we always said it before we hung up the phone. How many times my last words have been I love you-Oh Mommy you taught us so well!!

You let us set our own pace in school but if we started out with high grades we had better maintain them or lose privileges. But you never compared one of us to the other-you let us be individuals but standards were not lacking.

You taught us that God made all of us and color was not to be a gauge for anything except to love all people. You integrated the first bowling alley in Dayton when we took the news branch bowling and the man said Calvin could not bowl because he was black. You told him straight out "if he can't bowl here then no one else from the Dayton Daily News will ever bowl here again, we all bowled that day.

And when my Sunday School teacher brought me home one Sunday-weeks after I had taken a young man to church with me whose skin was darker you comforted me. She said to take me out of the church because at age 13 -I was being persecuted because I believed we were all the same. Persecution was a word I had never experienced -until Westwood Baptist Church members taught me firsthand what it was. You would not let me go back nor did I want to go.

But you loved me through the pain and reminded me of the angel on my shoulder. I heard that my whole life -even in a conversation we had the end of June this year. "I keep telling you honey, you have had an angel on your shoulder since you were a little girl. I have watched as he worked things out for you that would never work out for anyone else. I believe today God blesses you like He does, because you take care of me and love others like you do." Well, Mommy –I do not know why as rotten as I am-but I know I am blessed. I brought one of the angels from your jewelry box home with me. I wear it every day as a reminder –on my left shoulder. What a blessing to give a child!!!

You were so proud of us!! Stan as he began to work his bus route at Dayton Baptist Temple!! With a bus that was always overflowing-and needed a 2nd bus to bring all the kids in. And Jerry, when he came home with his face beaming -after enlisting for the army. "Look Mom-No Record!! You hugged him so tight. He went to Vietnam as a Military Policeman!! And when he went to work for the Sheriff's Department after he came home we were all so proud!!

The police had always been a presence as we grew up. We learned early to respect authority and be grateful for their protection. With you having to go to the restaurant very early to get the coffee urns started–there was always a police cruiser at the Texaco station across the street. They waited until we were on the way to school before pulling away unless there was an emergency. How many trips I made to Winters Bank downtown to make Liz's deposit from the restaurant-scared to death, only to learn months later –there was always a plain clothes officer following me. Today if I come across an officer or a military person -I feel compelled to say thank you for what you do and let them know I pray for them. Because of your lessons!!

There are so many sweet memories. What fun we had when you and Bobby and I went to Gatlinburg!! You always made sure no matter what we did –that we enjoyed life. You taught us to laugh and to love and we may not have had a lot of material things growing up but we always had love. Plenty of love.

Mommy –our lives are changed forever –they will never be the same without you-but they are better because of you. You were always independent and worked hard to raise us and ask for no help, except from God. Now you are resting with the One in whom you trusted all those years. I told someone the other day you were probably telling someone up there "I can do it myself." That independence carried us through some hard times but it taught each of us we could do anything we set our minds to do. You repeated many times as we grew up-it is better to aim at something and miss than not aim at all. You taught each of us to always give more than was expected –no matter what the task at hand. Life lessons we will never forget.

I am grateful God prepared a house for Bobby Joe and I for 14 years and for you the last 25 years of your life. God had everything planned. We enjoyed many good times there. You had your own home, no rent and no worries -thanks to the help of my precious brothers -for the first time in years -you were able to relax. But you insisted on paying your own utilities-Miss independent and I will do it myself!!

I thank God every day for you finally accepting the fact an alert button was a necessity. It allowed us to all be together with you before you left for Heaven. Even though you were in hospice. The Lord worked it out for us. I will never forget asking you on Friday if you wanted anything. And that reply -no you had what you wanted-all 3 of your children together. And Jerry saying that was a bad way to get us together Mom. But what better way to be together than with our Mother? Just loving you and looking after you for a while. You spent your entire life looking after us-with a love and devotion not many have!! It was not the best of times for you –but you still had your sharp mind and knew us all. When I had to go back to Georgia early for payroll and asked you on Saturday if it was okay for me to home Sunday, you said yes. Stan said she means Georgia and you said I KNOW where she lives. Days that we will remember and cherish.

We will see you in Heaven Mommy with Bobby Joe and so many others who have gone on before. When we get there –we will never have to long to hear your voice again or shed another tear-because we miss you and we all miss you, every single day. But we thank God for giving us to you, our special, special Mother. There will never be another like you!!

With all my love,
Jerry Lee

In Loving Memory of Morris Lamb

He was a brother and a friend, with a heart of purest gold,
How many people he cared for- can never here be told.
He touched so many lives for the short time he spent on earth-
Just taking care of others –he could never have known his worth.
He was a tenderhearted man –by his looks you could not tell-
But as he spent time doing for others-his spirit would never fail.
Always doing his very best –even putting his own needs aside-
He did all he undertook so well –and in his work took pride.
He'd say "I'm here to take care of you guys
and Mike" and did the job so well.
To imagine not seeing him again in this life-is the hardest thing to tell.
A friend in time of trouble who was always there when you'd call,
Who never was too busy –even when the orders were tall.
He could look at a project and imagine an unseen beauty there -
And build anything without a plan –and made it with such care.
He was at ease with his music, as the guitar he would play-
And just as much at home in a boat-fishing, the very next day.
He had an unseen talent hidden well behind that smile -
Who would have known –he'd be gone in such a short while?
He spent his last hours in a place he loved to be-
In the ocean, on a boat, watching the fish at sea.
To say that we will miss him is an understatement it's true.
Just wish we could tell him one more time
"Morris, we love you".

Given to me by the Lord 10/3/2015
Jerry L Schock
Gal 6:2

In Loving Memory of our Sister Linda Garcia

She hurt so many times, she lived with so much pain
but her faith remained so strong, time and time again.
She trusted in the Lord, knowing He was in control,
no matter what the problem, off her back it would roll.
She was a sister tried and true, no matter what the need
you could depend on her to always take God's lead.
The pain is now behind her as she stepped on Heaven's shore
and saw our Blessed Saviors face and peace forevermore.
Oh Lord You know we'll miss her each and every day.
As we trust in You alone to take the pain away.
Sometimes we would call with nothing much to say
-except I'm checking on you and have a brighter day.
She fought a long hard battle now she's finished her race
-She's resting in the arms of Jesus in that very special place.
One day we'll be together praising our precious Lord
as we rest on Heaven's shore
To spend eternity with our loved ones who
have all gone on before.

Our lives have been changed forever -we will miss you.
Given to me by the Lord Jerry Lee Schock
April 12, 2021

It Seems So Soon

It seems too soon my brother, for you to be going Home,
But we pray your crossing is easy –and know you'll not be alone.
For Jesus is waiting on the other side –to take you safely there,
To a place with no more pain or sorrows and never any care.
We hate to let you go now but we know it is in God's time-
And we would not have you suffer –even though we're left behind.
You're leaving us such sweet memories of good times we have shared,
And the thing we'll remember most, is just how much you've cared.
We will miss your great hugs each time we would meet-
All the conversations we shared and then that smile so sweet.
Our one true consolation is that we had love to share-
And know that someday in Heaven we'll all be meeting there.

For our sweet brother Roy,
as we wait on the Lord.
Jerry L Schock
10/12/14

Thank you Lord for letting me hear his voice today
and tell him how much I love him -
and hear him say I love you too sis-like he always
did. You let me read this poem to him.
Even though he is weak Lord-You sustain life
until You are ready to come for him.

I've Watched You

I've watched you - oh so many times, with a smile upon your face,
Hiding tears and pain inside - covered only by His grace.
The pain you hide so well within, as you see a loved one leave,
May be hidden from the world - but I still see the grief.
So I ask the Father draw you close to Him -with comfort all around
Wrap you in His arms of love - and with angels -you - surround.
Another now is free from pain -and finally she's at rest,
I can almost see the Father - draw her close to His breast-
And hear Him welcome her to Heaven -and the joy bells as they ring-
Hush !! I hear a heavenly choir - can you hear her as she sings?
With trouble gone - the tears are dried-no more will she feel pain-
This earthly vessel of clay gone home -will never hurt again.
She's waited- like us- for the promise-of a meeting on that shore-
Where, when we get to Heaven - there's parting, nevermore.

For Miss Bertha
- In loving memory of Faye
By Jerry L. Schock

Mothers

Mothers are God's gift to enrich our lives and help us as we grow,
The pain of losing our special friend is much harder than we know.
They're our help in times of trouble and encourage us on the way.
They teach us all about the Lord and from them we learn to pray.
A mother shows us by her faith, what a godly woman should be,
They love us through childhood, when we're grown they set us free.

We'll miss Granny's quiet spirit and seeing that precious smile,
As she sat and listened to the man of God, preaching for a while.
We'll miss her tender -hearted ways and just knowing she was here,
In the midst of all the hurt and pain, will bring us peace and cheer.
The seat beside you may be empty and although it will be strange,
In time you'll find the peace, that our loss is truly Heaven's gain.

She has hurt so much in recent days and now she'll suffer no more,
As she walks the streets of Heaven with those who've gone before .
Granny must have watched from up above and I'm sure she smiled again,
Knowing that even in the midst of death - others were led to Him.
What a precious memory the Lord has given to those she left behind,
We praise our Heavenly Father, who even in death is so kind.

So hold on my precious sister and rest in Jesus' arms for a while,
Until you're able to walk on your own, and really want to smile.
Our prayers will bring you comfort as the angels surround you today,
And bear you up in arms of love, as you journey on your way.
Remember in the darkest of nights, when the pain is hard to bear,
God touches an intercessor –to hold you up in prayer.

Given to me by the Lord 2/21/10
Jerry Schock

My Heart Cries Out

Oh how my heart cries out for you - as I petition God above,
To fill your life with peace, and surround you with His love.
I know behind the smile- there you hide the tears,
And the pain I've seen you suffer through - these past few years.
Yes, time will bring relief-as it has healed before,
And God will ease the pain, and bring you peace once more.
But oh my precious sister, what a testimony I see!!!
As you walk through each valley -and send to Him your plea.
You still can laugh and sing, and praise the Father above,
You will never ever know how much, you manifest His love.

Written in loving memory of Faye
by Jerry L. Schock

My Heart Is Heavy

Father my heart is heavy, and yet I still rejoice,
As I watch those in the valley, I listen to Your voice.
You've promised in the valley , we will never walk alone.
You tell us You will never leave us on our own.
The trials will come our way, as we're on this road of life,
but we know that there will be victory from the strife.
As I pray for those in the valley, I plead for peace and grace,
Keep them calm and fill them with your love in this place.
Show them that the mountaintop is waiting up ahead,
And as long as You are with us, nothing we should dread.
As we are in the valley, we know You've gone ahead,
You know each rock and stony place where we must tread.
You have cleared the way before as we are going through,
And promise You will be there, so we can lean on You.

By Jerry L Schock
Given to me by the Lord

One Day

One day in Heaven our Father looked to the earth below;
And told another child to make the crossing I know.
His soft voice spoke the words; it's time to come on home.
But rest assured those left behind will never be alone.
The Father sends His angels to guide you on your path,
Until sweet peace will fill your soul-and ease your mind at last.
There will always be an empty place – deep within your heart-
But very soon you'll find – we'll never be apart.

Jerry L Schock

Our Hearts Are Broken

Although our hearts are broken
and we cannot understand-
We still know our Father in
Heaven has a Master plan.
One of the hardest things we'll
ever do is lay a child to rest-

Yet deep within our sorrow
we know we have been blessed.
Our hearts are crying out in
pain to our Father up above-
Surround this precious family
and let them feel Your love.

Heaven must have needed an angel
and Jesus called her home-
Now we're left to wonder how
we'll ever make it alone.

But Father You see much farther
than we can ever see-
So help us as we lean on You –
dear Father is our plea.

Given to me by the Lord as
you walk this road of pain –
with much love and prayer
Miss Jerry
April, 2004

Our Mother's

Our Mother's are so special to us-
each and every day,
And our hearts can feel so broken
when they are called away.
Heaven surely needed another rose –
to brighten the garden there-
So the Father called her home –
to a place with no more care.
Someday we'll make the crossing –
and find her on that shore-
And we will praise the Lord together –
and shed our tears no more.

With much love and Prayer -in the homegoing of
your Mother-
Jerry L Schock
4/13/08

Remembering Theresa Beuchler

1/25/2009

Dear Lord You know we'll miss her and her precious smiling face,
She surely was our special angel-overflowing with grace.
The smallest gift would bring a smile and fill her with such cheer,
And then you could see that grin- spreading from ear to ear
Even in the midst of pain she had in times gone past-
She'd praise Your precious Name-and say it will not last.
She had a great sense of humor and laughter came easy to her.
She loved the Lord and people-that you knew for sure.
When she graduated to Heaven with Jesus holding her hand,
The faith she had became sight –there in glory land.
The pain is gone and the smile wide as she greets loved ones there-
Praising the Lord for all He's done and His tender, loving care.
Even though we miss her and our hearts are filled with pain-
In just a little while we know, we all will meet again.

For the family of Theresa Buechler
Given to me by the Lord
Jerry L Schock
2/29/2012

She Went to Sleep

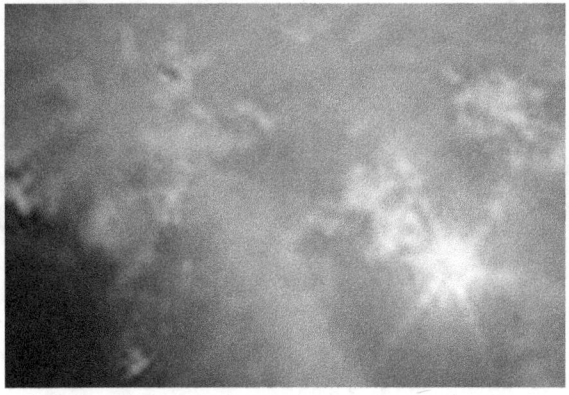

She went to sleep on earth last night,
but in Heaven she awoke;
Even though you will miss her –
even though your hearts are broke,
You know with the Heavenly choir –
today your sister will sing;
Throughout the streets of Heaven –
her angel voice will ring.
The Father's made a promise,
one day we'll meet again,
The time we all look forward to –
though we cannot know just when.
I've watched as time and again
you've seen a loved one go home,
Depending on God for all the peace-
you'd never find alone.
I am grateful for His love,
that truly will sustain,
All whom she will leave and
those who must remain.

By Jerry L. Schock
10-6-98

She's Gone On

She's gone on to glory and we are left alone-
But part of us is still at peace knowing she's at home.
Far from all she suffered, and far from sickness and pain;
It truly is our loss but-most surely Heaven's gain.
I hear her sweet voice singing I can see the lights of home-
And close my eyes and envision our Father on the throne.
Today she sees things clearer than she's ever seen before-
For today she closed her eyes here
and woke on Heaven's shore.

For Miss Bertha 's family from Miss Jerry
02/26/07

Someone to Lead

We needed someone to lead us and guide us on the way,
One who could take us –through even the hardest day.
So God made that special someone who is like no other;
This blessing we've been given –He chose to call our Mother.
She seems to have an answer to every question we ask,
And never seems to tire-no matter how hard the task.
Sometimes she's a nurse-who treats our hurts and pain-
At other times she's a manager without a thing to gain.
Sometimes she's a maid or cook –it seems there is no end-
But always she is the one on whom we can depend.
She does not demand any wages and her schedule is not set-
She serves at the oddest hours and never seems to forget.
She lives to serve her family and has a very full life-
Being a Mother and a friend and also being a wife.
She loves the Lord and church –knows many hymns by heart.
She's always ready to serve no matter how small the part.
Today is the time to honor, God's special gift from above-
By giving back to our Mother's, an extra measure of love.

Happy Mothers Day -
2007
Jerry L Schock

Sympathy Short Poems

Someday there will no tears fall from our eyes- No pain will break our hearts
When we meet our blessed Savior in the skies-
Where from loved ones, we'll never part.

The place your loved one moved to, is still to us unknown,
But surely he was ready, his body, weary had grown.
One day we'll cross the river – into a land that now seems far- And
know the truth he now sees, as we join the brightest Star.

For Bill Sweat in the
homegoing
of his father
3/10/97
Jerry L Schock

The Burden

The burden is too great my Lord-no daylight I can see
The valley is too deep – please come and rescue me!!
Each time my heart cries out – faithful You've always
been- Dear Father here I am –praying once again.
I do not understand why others suffer so-
It may be precious Father -I'm not supposed to know-
For each time You bring a burden –or someone suffers pain;
It draws me to reach out to them – in prayer once again.
You've touched my heart so many times, I felt that it would break
As other's burdens I've tried to bear –and intercession make.
Another precious one is hurting in their heart-
As one they held so dear –from this earth did part.
Strengthen them dear Lord, as only You can do,
Surround them now with angels and draw them close to You.
Let them know the burden is carried to Your throne,
By many who love them –don't let them feel alone.

Jerry Schock
11-20-99

The Burden is Heavy

We cannot carry the burden Lord – it is too hard we plea –
Hold on my precious child–this care was meant for me.
The burdens of those we love are sent from God above,
For us to carry together – in splendid Christian love.
A burden is so hard to bear when we try to carry it alone,
And so the Father sent the Son –and angels from the throne.
They come through a smile, a hug or even a special touch –
But all are sent from Heaven –to those we love so much.

> Galatians 6:2
> By Jerry L Schock
> 8/24/02

The Garden

There is a garden up in Heaven,
With a gate we cannot pass through,
Until the time arrives, Jesus calls for me and you.
Our loved one has gone on, and we feel so alone
But the Heavenly Father never leaves us on our own. His
love will sustain us in the painful days to come,
He bears the burden with us-one day we will go home.
Forever we'll be united with those we hold so dear; Until then the
Father is waiting to dry our every tear. May His love sustain and
keep you until again, we meet; As I pray for peace and comfort –
kneeling at Jesus feet.

Jerry L Schock

The Homegoing

Another beautiful angel, just entered Heavens gate.
But Lord, we miss her so, why could You not wait? She's
mine now, My dear child, I needed her with Me.
Her body no longer suffers, I set her spirit free.
She brought you joy for just a while-I left her there 'tis true.
I had to let you see just how much I really love you.
I know your heart is broken and the pain it goes so deep-
But this was my own special rose, I could not let you keep.
She was sent to brighten up your world, so often filled with care;
Now she rests within My arms, as you and I, the pain will share.
I'll carry you My child, until the peace will come,
You never will forget her, then one day I'll call you home-
Tears will become a memory, as will the pain you feel today-
But remember I have promised I will be with you always.

Psalm 34:18 91:11,12
Jerry L Schock

The Long Road

It's been such a long road, full of so much pain,
And yet I know my sister has only Heaven to gain.
She'll win the battle she has fought, no matter how it ends,
Should You decide to heal her, or life come to an end.
Her faith is like a candle, lighting all she's near-
Her voice is filled with calmness-never doubt or fear.
Her life has been a light for all the world to see-
No matter what the path it took-she saw the victory.
She's prayed so many times for You to heal her Lord,
So she might continue on, spreading Your Holy word.
But Father, life is slipping oh too fast away-
And yet she's looking forward to a brighter day.
Wrap her in Your arms of love, as she nears that shore-
Hold her close and comfort her-as angel's guide her o'er.

Psalm 23 For Miss Johnnie
Given to me by the Lord 5/9/2000
Jerry L Schock

The Loved One's He Has Taken

The loved one's He has taken, to glory up above;
Leave our lives so empty and longing for their love.
But we know beyond all doubt, waiting on a distant shore,
That our precious loved one, will suffer nevermore.
You've seen your closest friends and a son's precious wife,
Joining our Father in Heaven -called away from this life.
And yet you stand before Him -though wounded as a bird;
Singing His glory and praise, like I have never heard!
The hurt within your heart -is hidden from many eyes;
But I can see it - yes my precious sister, I do realize.
It is at a time like this, when there is nothing one can say;
All I can do for you is send many prayers, Heaven's way.
I know that time will help heal, some of the hurt and pain;
But only God in Heaven - sees you suffer, time and again.
I'm asking for those angels- to surround you with His love;
To guide each step you take - from Heaven up above.
I ask for your protection - and a peace beyond all measure;
For in you, I see my sister, a very special treasure.
Someday very soon-we'll join our loved one's there-
And thank the Father above-we'll never have a care.

In loving memory of Faye
Miss Jerry

The Pain, The Peace

Father, how we hurt inside, when a loved one goes away,
And we are left behind to cope, with each new passing day.
Sometimes we cry and even smile, remembering things they have done;
Inside our hearts they are alive, we can't believe, they're gone.
Death is one thing in this life, where we have no control;
It is the time we wonder, will I ever again be whole?
Our spirits and our hearts, cry out to You in pain;
Oh please, my Heavenly Father, take away the rain.
Let me see the sun shine, for just a little while,
Send quickly to my face, the sweetness of a smile,
For the only victory I have found, as I travel through this life,
Is the victory You have given, in the middle of my strife.
You know my heart is aching, You see the tears I shed,
You know that so very deep within, there are things I dread. But
today my Heavenly Father, Your Presence will be so real,
As around my very being, Your own arms, I feel.
Yes today I will find comfort and peace will not escape;
Because You walk beside me, with every step I take.

Psalm 23
by Jerry L. Schock
7-24-98

The Path

The path is rough and stony, I cannot go on alone, I said.
Come on my precious child, there is nothing to fear, for I have gone ahead.
But Lord, the way is strange to me, I fear the dark, I dread,
Hold on my precious child, for by My own hand, you will be led,
Oh Father, I feel so alone, without my loved one near.
I know My precious child, but I needed them to be here.
I feel the pain burning deep within, when from loved ones you must part;
But 'til you can see the light ahead, I'll hold you closer to My own heart.
Please trust in Me, My dear child, I know what's best for you;
I see much farther down the road than anyone it's true,
I know the questions in your mind and know you wonder why.
But just stay close to Me, My child, each teardrop I will dry.
Someday you will understand, when life on earth will end;
Then in My presence you will find, I am your dearest friend.

Given me to by the Lord
Jerry Lee Schock
7/24/98

The Struggle

Oh Lord we grow so weary from the struggle of it all-
As the fiery darts of Satan round us we see fall.
He plans to undo our peace and plays games with our minds-
We seem to struggle daily not to get behind.
We're standing in the gap as you walk a rocky road-
The Lord sent us especially to help you bear the load.
He's walking right beside us as the journey we begin-
And rest assured He'll be there well beyond its end.
He lets us know when you're hurting or need an extra prayer-
And from the throne of Heaven sends angels waiting there.
So if you feel a touch upon your cheek today –
It's the finger of the angels God is sending you way.

Jerry L Schock

The Whisper of Her Wings

Such a gentle breeze is blowing, across this place today-
It's the angel wings of your loved one-who to Heaven flew away.
She's resting now with Jesus and is waiting for you there- You
have the sweet assurance- she's forever in His care.
She's met the other loved ones who've gone on before-
As she made the crossing where she'll live forevermore.
Rest now in the promise of the Savior we hold dear-
Even though you miss her – there is nothing you should fear.
Just as she crossed over on the journey to Heaven above-
You'll someday make that crossing to live forever in His love.

Jerry L Schock
10-1-96

Their Sacrifice

If there would be one prayer I'd pray
It's for peace and joy along the way
For missionaries who serve and love You Lord
As they work to preach Your precious Word
They give it all and then move far away
From home and friends for many a day
Leave behind a life of ease and all the comfort we know
And off to a foreign place they go
To follow Your will and preach the Word
Many times with nothing but You Lord.
Protect them and provide for each and every need
For every missionary now-dear Lord I plead.

Given to me by the Lord 06/18/06
Jerry L Schock

There's A Road Ahead

There's a road ahead that's dreaded without the one we love;
But soon we know You'll take her, to live in Heaven above,
Our hearts are fearful dear Lord, to think of life alone;
And now we must confess we fear what is unknown-
You've given her more time than we ever thought You'd give
As we held her close in prayer and love-just hoping she would live
But as time is growing shorter and we know she is in pain
We have to ask You Father-what is there to gain?
But deep inside we know it's all within Your Hand
And tho' we can't comprehend-it is part of Your plan.

For Miss Bertha's family
From Miss Jerry
02/25/07

To Comfort You In Sorrow

When a loved one leaves this earth
And we're feeling all alone-
Walking down a dreary path,
So dark and yet unknown.
The road ahead may not be easy-
Rocky places many it's true-
But I'm trusting He'll place angels-
On every side of you.
The pain you feel He surely knows
And understands today.
But He will help you bear the load-
He's allowed to come your way.
Comfort and peace may seem far-
But His promises are there.
He'll never leave or forsake us- And He does truly care.

Jerry L Schock
Given to me by the Lord
2-2-97

Tomorrow or Today

Don't worry about tomorrow, live only for today,
God has not promised tomorrow –it is just His way.
We have no earthly power over what the future will be,
Just put your trust in Him who always holds the key.

The unknown frightens us, for within our finite minds,
We have no power to understand-it is all in His time.
He holds our future in His hands and our needs today-
Just take the burden to Him-and at His feet let it stay.

When we worry and fret over a future that may not be,
We say we cannot trust He can care for you and me.
Worry slanders every promise God has ever made,
The altar is where it belongs-the price is already paid.

So if today you feel unsure of what the future will be,
Remember who holds tomorrow for both you and me.
Take all cares to the Lord as you wait upon His will,
Rest assured His answer, is always "peace, be still".

*Inspired by Pastor Rex McPherson's words to
a hurting Sister in Christ.
From the Lord's heart to mine.
Jerry L Schock
11/8/14*

James 4:14 Whereas ye know not what shall be on the morrow. For what is your life? It is even a vapour, that appeareth for a little time, and then vanisheth away.

We Said Goodbye

Today we said goodbye to a precious sister here-
And though our hearts are sad, and we shed a tear –
You've given us the promise we will meet again,
Lord, help us to remember that in the end, we win.
As she made her journey to Heaven, in the angels care-
Jesus held her hand to usher her over there.
She is safe and free from pain, with her Savior now,
We will have the strength, to make it through somehow.
Heaven really isn't far and the time is drawing near,
When we will leave this world and our hearts will fill with cheer

Given to me by the Lord,
In loving memory of Miss Theresa
3/1/2012

Psalms 116:15

"Precious in the sight of the LORD is the death of his saints."

What A Precious Angel

What a precious angel You sent to bless us Lord-
As Bertha sang and praised You in song, and thru the Word-
Her voice is stilled on earth but in Heaven she still sings
You took our precious loved one-home on angel wings.
She wanted to be with you-but she still wanted to stay-
Please don't let her suffer Lord-we all came to pray.
She spent some time here- with Your angels in her room-
They brought to her Your promises that death
need not mean gloom.
She lingered between life and making her journey home-
But in Your grace and goodness –she left us so alone.

In loving memory of Miss Bertha,
03/18/07

When We Can Do No More

At times Lord the burden is so great we cannot even pray-
We long within our hearts to see the sunshine's ray.
We ask You move the clouds and take away the rain-
Take us from the valley and make us whole again.
Then suddenly without warning, You move the clouds away-
You show us by Your loving Hand-the light of a brand new day-
You send a special unexpected blessing from Heaven up above-
And shower us in that blessing with care and peace and love.
If only we could learn to let go of the heavy load-
And trust in your provision as we walk a rocky road-
By letting go and letting God we learn the lesson anew-
That the only thing that will never change, is our love from You.
So the next time there is a valley that seems too deep and wide-
Remind us precious Lord –that You are by our side.
The only thing you ask is faith and our full trust in You-
Help us to remember Lord-Your promises are true.

Given to me by the Lord for my sister, Linda
Jerry L Schock
4/20/13
Heb. 13:15 for he hath said,
I will never leave thee, nor forsake thee

With Deepest Sympathy

No one can really understand or know the pain you feel,
But the Lord above in Heaven, who can, and surely will.
Sometimes in this life there are valleys we must go through,
But I know our Lord and Savior, is watching over you.
In His word He gives the promise, of angels to protect,
And the Holy Spirit to guide us, we know He won't forget.
The pain that is inside you, the world may never see,
It hides behind the smile you wear, but cannot be hidden from me.
My heartfelt prayers go out to you, as another cross you bear,
And I pray that it will help you, to know how much I care.
There are no words in this world, to bring you comfort now;
But I pray that guardian angels will hover near somehow.
And spread their wings around you, until your pain has passed;
And give you blessed peace and consolation at last.

Psalm 91:1,2,4,11,12
By Jerry L. Schock

With Heartfelt Sympathy

There is little that anyone can do and less that one can say
But ask the Lord to comfort you as you walk this road today.
No one can really understand the pain that you will bear,
But I pray somehow it comforts you to know that other's care.
And knowing in those tear-filled days that you still must face,
Our Father up in Heaven, will send an extra measure of grace.
Without your precious loved one to help you through the day,
The Lord will send His angels to guide you on the way.
In His words He gives the promise of angels to protect,
And the Holy Spirit to guide us, we know, He won't forget.
Know that many prayers will be sent to the Father above,
Asking Him to send His angels and surround you with His love.

Psalm 91:1,2,4,11,12
Given me by the Lord,
September 7, 1996
Jerry L Schock

Wits End

I am at my wits end Lord, there is nothing more I can do,
Except to put my faith and all my trust in You.
This child is far away from where my dreams would have them be;
Wandering in the wilderness-help them Lord I plea!
Fear creeps in as I wonder –how long suffering You'll be.
Plant hedges all around them -protect with all Your might.
As they linger in the darkness-until they can see the light.

As we wait upon the Lord
Deut. 32:11
Jerry L Schock

My Journey Thus Far

God is allowing my story to be told in print with this book.

When Mom and Dad were first divorced my Grandma Herman told Mom she could not raise us alone. Grandma told her to put us in the children's home and Mom said no. She said she would raise us no matter how many jobs it took She always said she was not raising us alone-God was watching over us.

For a while we stayed with Grandma and Grandpa Herman. Since I was the first granddaughter and born on Grandpa's 77th birthday-he favored me. Every Saturday morning, he and I would walk down the back alley the several blocks to Andy's Market. I loved garlic bologna and he would buy me a ring of garlic bologna and get his block of limburger cheese. Mom loved that too, but I could never even taste it. On the way home we would stop at the Texaco station and he would get me a chocolate bar. We would sit at that big kitchen table he had built-being a carpenter by trade- and he would get the saltine crackers, cut up the bologna for me and then start on his cheese. Grandpa loved the Cincinnati Red's baseball team and we would watch it on TV-him in his easy chair-me at his feet and his parakeet, Petey on his head. Good memories.

We later moved to Parkside homes and on Sunday-Mom would put my youngest brother in the stroller-Stan behind him -and I would hold onto the bar. We would walk across the grassy area to the Lutheran church for Sunday School. As we got older, we moved closer to downtown Dayton and the 3 of us would walk to the City Mission for Sunday School. Hobart and Thelma Roark handled services there. They owned a fur shop and furniture store in Laura, OH., and went to Westwood Baptist Church.

Thelma took an interest in me and Mom would let her take me on Friday and stay with them until after church Sunday. Saturday we would go for a walk and then back home to eat and clean up. Then to the furniture store where she played the piano or organ and I would sing. The manager, Dick Foreman taught me how to greet customers. My first exposure to what became my career, the furniture business.

Saved at age 13 at the Westwood Baptist Church in Dayton, I wanted to tell everyone how to get saved. Mom worked at the YMCA as a cashier in the cafeteria and had exchange students from the Dominican Republic. I invited Ramon Diaz to church. Taking my first visitor to church felt good, UNTIL we got into the church. 63 years later I STILL remember the cold feeling going down that aisle -it was as if someone poured a tray of ice over the entire church! All because his skin was darker. After quite a while my Sunday School teacher took me home and told Mom to pull me out of the church because I was being persecuted as I thought everyone should be treated the same My heart was broken but I determined to become a Missionary nurse and go to Africa so I could spread the gospel.

We were raised to believe the color of one's skin had nothing to do with anything-we did not know the word prejudice. We all went to school together from grade school through high and wondered what the big deal was when in the early 60's they said the schools in Dayton were to be integrated-we had always been together. My best friend all the way through school was Virginia Glanton, a black girl. Mom said you could cut anyone and we ALL would bleed red. Mom had a Dayton Daily Newspaper branch as one of her 3 jobs and we had a bowling team and a baseball team. One Saturday morning Mom took us bowling for the news branch to a bowling alley on Brown Street. One of our carriers was Calvin Jones -a black boy-and the manager of the bowling alley pointed at him when we went in to get our shoes and said "he can't bowl here". But Mom said, "if he can't bowl then none of us will and NO ONE from the Dayton Daily News will ever bowl here again". Needless to say we ALL bowled- and integrated that bowling alley then and there!

Even though I found another church it was not the same –I graduated from Stivers High School high school in 1961 -10th in a graduating class of 161. Two highlights in school were the lead part I had in "Oklahoma" and the Bible Club teacher asking me to speak. When asked what I wanted to speak on I said faith and she wrote the word acrostically and it said Forsaking All I Take Him. I have never forgotten it.

I started nurses training at Miami Valley Hospital and during my first year-allowed a man 8 years older than myself to take advantage of me. Thank God He forgives our failures when we confess and ask. Although Doug did all he could to make me lose my baby he failed. He got married the day before we were to be. Unmarried and pregnant-I turned to my best friend-Mom. When I called and told her she just said, "you better pack your clothes and come home".

Bobby Joe was born November 14, 1962. We lived at home for a few years and then moved to West Carrollton, OH. with a friend who had a son the same age as Bobby. We eventually got our own apartment and I bought a car. When the job at Penker Construction ended, I went around the corner to Roberts furniture to apply for a job-where they sold everything for the home. Howard Smith gave me a customer to see what I could do and when I sold a pair of lamps, hired me-saying if I could sell accessories, I could sell anything. Worked there until the owner bankrupted the company and moved back to Kentucky. In 1971, Ken Fletcher, Howard Smith and Don Wright bought the bankrupt stock. Ken called and asked if I wanted to come back to work-said Smitty told him if they were to succeed -they needed me. Of course, I did!! We could not afford a new sign so changed the name from ROBERTS to ROBERDS -switching the *T to a D* and thus Roberds Furniture was started.

Over time we had a total of 28 stores/distribution centers in 4 states and except for two in GA -I was instrumental in opening all of them as corporate coordinator. I was in FL opening 2 new stores when Bobby Joe was killed in a motorcycle wreck May 21, 1986. Neighbors said the police had been to the house God let me buy in 1974, several times to let me know and when they could not reach me, called my brother Jerry-whom they knew was a Deputy for Montgomery County. and he called my boss. Ken Fletcher did not know the Lord as far as I know but I prayed daily for him. He did not want me to talk about the Lord at work. Still He had my preacher come to the store to call me in Florida to let me know. God had already arranged things as He always does.

Mom had retired at age 65 on May 10th -her birthday- from the YMCA and Ken asked her at Bobby's funeral if she was going to move into my house- telling her I did not need it as I would be traveling. She said yes and Jerry moved her in June 1st. Mom lived there until she went home to be with the Lord July 19, 2011. After my move to Georgia the rent for the apartment plus a house payment was too much but both of my brothers offered to split the house payment and it was done 3 ways so Mom could stay where she was happiest.

I had asked to move to Florida in 1987 and continued to open stores between Georgia and Florida and Ohio. June of 1992, Ken called telling me we had stores in trouble in Georgia and he needed me to move there since I was the only one who could fix it. Serving and settled in my church-I told Ken I had to pray about it-I heard a gasp on the other end of the phone but that is all I can do when a decision is needed. He asked how long it would take to get an answer and I was confident God would let me know by Monday and told him so. He told me it would mean a $24000.00 a year salary but I had to be sure God was in the move not me. I prayed all weekend and only ask 2 things of the Lord so I would KNOW it was Him, not me. I said Lord please do not ever let me drive on I85 to get to work and not one dime will come out of my pocket to make the move (The company paid no expenses ahead of time). Monday, I called and asked the questions-they would get my apartment -pay first month's rent and deposit and all utility deposits would be made-close to the store. And, they would give me a check for the $3000.00 moving expense ahead of time. So, feeling confident it WAS God in charge-I said I would go-and he wanted me there in 3 weeks. I made some calls from the Shepherd's guide we had at church to see what churches were near Norcross and the first call was Galilean Baptist and 27 years later I am still there-God always knows where we belong, and I have never had to drive 85 or 285 to get to work. July 14, 1992, I moved my letter to Galilean and the 2nd week Ollie and Linda "adopted" me into their family. Linda's favorite saying is we are all kin under the skin. Even though they never met Mom they loved her and she loved them.

With the move to Georgia I uncovered over $450,000.00 that had been stolen from the company and we moved the thieves out. Taking over inventory control helped and by December we had 21 people behind bars for theft.

We continued to open stores in all markets as I traveled from Georgia to Florida to Ohio. In 1996 we opened Roberds Grand in Cincinnati, Ohio. -a megastore-nearly 6 acres, larger than Riverfront Stadium.

I lived in the apartment until 1997 and signed the papers on my birthday to buy a condo-after the apartment owners wanted to raise the rent over $100.00 per month. I saw an ad for a realtor on TV and called Sherrell to ask where she went to church. She told me and asked why? I explained God knew where I needed to be but if she did not know Him she could not listen to Him. It was clear God let me know I could spend $60,000.00 for a condo and she told me I would never find one for that. I explained she could not nor could I- but He knew where it was and 22 years later, I am still here (price was $59,900.00).

After opening a Distribution Center in Georgia-we moved our appliance and furniture Customer Service teams there. Every morning some of us would meet in my office and pray for one another and the business. June of 1999, our CFO from corporate called and Bob said he understood I was having prayer meetings in my office. I said yes, he told me he loved me and I know he did-but he could not allow me to continue, etc. I told him if he took God's hand off the business, we would lose it and he said he could not help it-Dec. that year the company filed Chapter 13. By June, 2000, the liquidators were scheduled in and not wishing to watch nearly 30 years of my life's work torn apart-I took my 3 weeks vacation and resigned, without prospects. I went home and remember laying my keys on the coffee table and telling the Lord I NEVER wanted to be in the furniture business again. Three weeks later I was working for a computer company in Covington where one of my road techs had gone. By October it became evident there was something else awaiting and after praying about it I resigned.

Nov. 2000, a call came from one of young men that had been at Roberds and was now at the then Plan It Oak-asking if I was working-he said we have had the rest now want the best-they needed someone to run Customer Service. Nov 7th when I went to work there my entire work life changed for the better!! Thanksgiving meant the company provided meat and we all brought side dishes in for the meal. As we gathered in the break room at the warehouse-Mike Hall -the owner-asked if I would pray and ask for blessing over the food!! I was sure I had died and gone to Heaven!! In the nearly 18 years I worked -Mike and Tim encouraged me to pray-spread the gospel and lead our folks to the Lord. When Mike handed me my ring for 10 years of service-he kindly said, "If we have a spiritual leader-it is Jerry". I am truly blessed. Several young people will be in Heaven because of the freedom they gave me. I have thanked God many times for NOT listening to me. I finally retired Sept 2018.

One of most wonderful blessings going to work for Mike has been my "adopted" granddaughter Gladys Everson -she calls me Nana. Most of the kids at work still call me that. I am ever so grateful we did not learn prejudice growing up or I would have missed this sweet girl and the sisters God gave me at church.

All the wonderful names I have been called down through the years and the sweet things that have been said are flooding my mind. I remember Mom saying if you have something to do-do it today-tomorrow may not come. So here goes-As I have told everyone who was so complimentary all my life -ALL the glory belongs to the Lord-not me. I am rotten to the core. I remember Mom telling me when God made me-He threw the mold away because the world could not stand 2 of me. Well, I believe it. I have a big mouth. Bona Griffieth our designer told me I was one of the things they told her to watch out for when she was hired at Roberds, because I would try to get her saved. They did not know she was a Christian and the Lord worked it out she flew home with me when Bobby Joe died. HEY I LOVE that reputation and gladly claim it still today. even on the phone God gives me that boldness.

Bona sent me a sweet note after I returned to Florida to thank me for showing her faith. Then I got a wonderful letter from Travis Hudson, my Pastor at Moraine Heights Baptist Church. He said after nearly 40 years of preaching-he had never seen faith-until he saw it in me at Bobby's funeral and thanked me. Clemmon Chappell-one of our GPA preachers said I was his Epaphroditus -Rick Glass another GPA preacher-called me our GPA prayer warrior-Bro Dennis Harkins thanked me for being his and his wife's Barnabus. Bro Jim Moore called me a prophetess one morning as he asked I pray for his eye-and the Bro Tolbert Moore at his 90th birthday –was sitting next to a preacher across from me and said he always watched me during the service and if he saw my hand go up he knew the service was okay -if not he wondered what was wrong-because I knew how to get hold of the Holy Spirit. I love you ALL for those kind words.

ALL the glory belongs to Jesus!! I am just so grateful to KNOW why I am on this earth and He enables me to fulfill my commission. He put me here to be a good prayer warrior and an encourager (and He is continually adding to the 3 excel workbooks of names that are called in prayer every Saturday) and of course there is a daily list. Any good you see in me is the LORD. Thanks to ALL of you who allow me to pray for you and encourage you when you are in need. As long as God gives me breath I will continue on this journey of intercessory prayer and encouragement.

For His Glory
Gal 6:2
Miss Jerry

Why I Wrote the Book

Many ask why I wrote these books. First, God put me here to be a good prayer warrior and encourager. Poems provide encouragement. The journey to publishing, with God's leading, has not been a hard one. Mother told me from my teenage years there was an angel sitting on my shoulder and she had watched that angel work things out for me that would never work out for anyone else. Seeking God's will made each step much easier. Having been blessed for more than 60 plus years to write poetry for those the Lord sent my way who were hurting, the answer to the question is simply For God's Glory. One of the first people to encourage me to publish was my sister-in-law, Pat and I said "when God's ready I will." In January 2018 I began to seek God's leading on how to start the process. Thus my journey to become an author began. I started through my filing cabinet as much of the poetry had been printed, creating the documents to submit to the publisher. Since publishing April 14, 2018, royalties have gone to the GPA at Galilean Baptist Church In Lawrenceville, GA to support missionaries.

Proceeds Goes to

**The Gospel Preachers Association
at Galilean Baptist Church**
1390 Monfort Rd,
Lawrenceville, GA 30046, United States
770 995 7045

www.ingramcontent.com/pod-product-compliance
Lightning Source LLC
LaVergne TN
LVHW011739060526
838200LV00051B/3259